I WOULD LIKE TO BE

If I could be anything in the world, I would be...
A sunset so beautiful in the sky,
To rise and set and capture lover's eyes.

Or a star to shine so brightly in the night
To accompany the moon and planets.

Or a soft spring rain to fall down from the heavens,
Or a brisk autumn wind,
To blow fiercely against the gallant trees.

Or a swiftly flowing wave,
To crash against the shore in times of anger.

But most of all, I'd like to be,
A BIRD
To soar a thousand lands
And watch a thousand seas.

For I am me,
And I am free.

Poetry of Life

By
Grace Rice

2013 Copyright All Rights Reserved.

THE ROOM

The room is so dreary,
It gives me chills from head to toes.

It's filled with empty trays of food,
Ice pitchers melting in the afternoon sun.
Kleenex boxes scattered on shelves,
Empty chairs and unread books.

The lights flicker on and off
The window blinds are kept shut.

The unmade bed next to him lay,
With no one in it.
He sleeps unaware of the silence
That surrounds him.

Shadows of objects glow in my mind,
Bringing a frightening, yet beautiful feeling to mind.

He breathes hard and long,
Sending short cries of pain.
His mouth lay open, his head tosses
From side to side.

He looks so old in here, so different.
Like I've never seen him before.
He looks so forgotten, so distant.
Yet I know he is still with me.

AN UNFORGETTABLE NIGHT

There is no world sound...
Only the cry of the wind blowing on the trees,
The quiet fall of the leaves onto the ground.
And your voice whispering into my mind.

Last night was the most beautiful night ever seen.
The sky was full of stars;
So many you couldn't even count them all.
It was so tempting;
You wanted to reach for every one of them.
To find out what heaven is really like.
And to find out what life and death
Is really all about.

All the stars,
The dark sky lit by the shining moon,
The sound of nothing but the shuffle of your feet
Down an empty street.
Knowing this would all be gone by morning,
But wanting it to last forever.

So I reached for the stars,

Hoping, wishing
That you had been there to share
The beauty with me.

OUR MEMORIES

Our memories are beginning to build up.
Today I sat in your arms and watched football.
We teased and laughed and even compared smiles;
You know we never did find out
Whose smile was better?

Yesterday we talked, listening to the radio.
Outside we ran free and played like little children.

We build our memories like sand castles,
Our love like stacking blocks,
Things were so beautiful until...
My blocks fell down.

We can't build our love on memories;
Put them away in a dusty attic for mice to sleep on
And dust to collect.

We must build our love on what it is,
Not what we want it to be.

But what would I do

Without my untouchable memories of you?

THE FOG

The fog rises up around small feet,
The sound of your voice echoes softly
In my mind.

You slept in silence, I wept in yours.
We shared a laugh
And we shared a smile,
Yet, there's still so much more to be
shared.

The fog isn't eyes of fruit trees you
know.
It's just fog.
Dreary sometimes, but you never know
What it is trying to say.

I'd like to put it away in a box and
Save if for another day.

The misty cloud outside my window
passes by,
Goes on its way home,
Travelling slowly and gently
It annihilates all my old dreams.

Where have they gone?
Where have you gone?
Perhaps you journeyed beside the misty
fog of nothing,
On your way to nowhere.

WAVES OF LONELINESS

There is no world sound...
Only the chirping of crickets,
And the silence of the waves on a
crystal lake.

The lights of a small city in the distance
Reflect on the waters and land of my
dreams.

The clouds, like puffs of white lace,
With a touch of gray silence.

The night is warm, but the shadows of
darkness
Send slightly cold chills onto the once
abiding body.

My dream land, sit and dream away.
The only other thought on my mind is
you
Wishing you were here to share these
Beautiful moments with me.

NIGHT SOUNDS

It seems as though night sounds
Are blocking my thoughts.
The crickets chirping in the brush.

The birds singing their little ones to sleep.
Or just the hum of the entire orchestra of night sounds.
The moon shines a path
For all creatures to find their way.

I followed the moonlit path
And found you.

Now the moon fades away slowly,
Waiting for the daybreak.
The days hold no mysteries;
Only the night sounds.

Now I await the moon...
To follow its path, back to you.

WHERE IS MY HAPPINESS?

In the chilled body of February
The ground is still bitten
And trees are still naked
And the sun will peep out occasionally.

And now as I await the spring,
I also await the happiness.
The sun will shine
The trees will be clothed
And ground will be soft
And the spring rains will fall.

And among the cheeriness of April
I will find my happiness.
I will walk along forgotten beaches,
And harmonize with the twittering of birds.
I will dream in the garden surrounded
By fruits and flowers.

And then shall I find my happiness?
If not, when? Where? How?
Shall I ever fid the end of the suffering?
To the cold nights I cry myself to sleep,
To the days when the sun doesn't shine?
When?

When can I stop searching?

When will I find the key and open the door?

Perhaps in the starry nights of August. Perhaps.

THANK YOU

The sun came up
And the day began.
You were there to help me through
A new abiding day.

The day was bright
And so were you.
I was feeling alright.
You gave me a smile and the day went on,
Brighter and more beautiful than ever.

The sun went down
And so did I
And there you were again,
To carry me through the night.

So there was the night,
The night was dark, brave and gently;
Yet it was there.
It cried softly and to itself
And so did you and me.

The moon came out
And shone itself bright and proud.
I was watching and wondering
You were sitting quietly
How did you manage to conquer my fears and doubts?

There was one star left in the whole sky. One dream left; one mind lost, and one heart broken.

THE FANTASY CASTLE

I'd like to live in a place where I can dream.
I'd like to live in a fantasy castle.

In the long and winding corridors,
I could walk down and dream,
Continue out to the gardens to
Walk among the flowers.

Oh, the gardens of my castle
Are so very beautiful.
The fruit trees bring their freshest fruits,
The flowers bloom their brightest blooms.

I can sit in the gardens,
And build my own world of fantasy.
I could dream about things no one could know.

I could dream about places of paradise
My own private island
The smell of rain on Sunday morning.

I could dream about lands that no humans occupy,
Sleeping in honey fields,
Soaring over the ocean like a seagull.
But most of all I'd dream about you.

THE HURT

Oh, how I long for your company

The gentle wind opens its arms to protect me.
Perhaps to protect me from you. Why?
I hope you weren't planning on hurting me.

Oh, yet the hurt is never planned.

It comes unexpectantly, like a blizzard or a storm
And the snow from the blizzard comes down hard.
It howls and moans and makes endless pathways
To more hurt.

The storm will let up eventually,
The sun will shine

There will be crystal skies and enchanting moons.
There will be priceless sunsets made for only you and me.
And we will miss them all...

The storm has not let-up.
The hurt has not left
My freezing soul.

I need you. I want you. Why?

Why can't you let go of the anguish?
The frightened boy you are.
You can't let go of the spiced dreams
And let your whispering feelings
Dance in your mind.

Only for a while.
Hold them for a while.

ABOUT YOU

Your eyes are the kind that can look right
Through a person.
They show a certain warmth,
That makes you seem so gentle.

And as I watch the cold and silver moon,
You only come passing through my mind.
Pausing briefly for a moment
The thought it brings makes me smile.

I demur for one more precious moment,
And listen to the rain breathe gently.
The cold and freezing wind blows gently
On the eyes of fruit trees.

You can be so warm at times
Like gentle flowing water.
And you can be so frightening at times
Like hot boiling waves.

Yet you are beautiful to me, so special!

I have so much more to learn about you,
I guess you like to keep secret things
About you locked up.

And let me search for the key.

Perhaps as I look into the sky at the stars,
I shall search for the key to
Open your heart
And discover your secrets.

DREAMS

The dreams,
All the haunting dreams,
All the wonderful dreams.

All shattered,
Like a large glass mirror
Placed perfectly on the wall.
The pieces; the little pieces
Somewhat like a jigsaw puzzle.

Who can put the pieces back together?

The mirror was once so lovely,
I could look at the girl inside and smile,
Laugh or cry. Once I could.
Once it was lovely.
I tried so hard for things I could never
      have.

Searched for things hidden in dark
      corners,
And a lost star in the night.
I searched; I tried to fit the pieces
      together.
I couldn't!

Now so much more is left to me.
I think I can find the star.
Yet, I still journey and travel

Down endless roads and forgotten
    paths.

But I shall find my star.
Somehow, someday,
I will find my dream.

HOW THINGS WERE

How sad it was,
How bad is seems
Just because of my long lost dreams.

I looked for you,
But you weren't there.
Our love was once
So very rare.

When things were dark,
I searched for light.
When things were wrong,
I thought they were right.

My dreams are lost.
I have no hope.
My life is gone,
I just can't cope.

INCOMPLETE

Whatever it is that makes me feel this
      way,
Tell it to go away.
Please make it go away.

There's a feeling of incompleteness,
Like a beautiful wrapped box with no
      bow.
There's so much missing, too much lost.
I don't know what but
I wish it would stop.

Too much is happening inside
to let anything happen outside.
It's like a scale of lead and feathers.
It's incomplete, unbalanced, lost.

Am I lost or is it just my dreams?
Are you really there or am I just
      imagining it?
Is there any hope for us, any
      understanding?

We have to fill those empty spaces;
Balance our scale of love.
We've got to try harder to fine...

Understanding, forgiveness,
A reality in ourselves

Before we search for them
in each other.

NEWNESS

A feeling of newness awakens me
from my sleep,
from my long lost dreams.
They are shattered and torn,
Never to return
Never to haunt me.

I have learned so much.
The rain falls outside my window,
with such a wonderful special sound.
The bough of the tree hangs onto the
      sky,
only to bring eerie shadows to my view.

The chilled and freezing winds,
replace the vanishing summer sun.
and all around a freshness has arisen.

The melting memories of my dream
      world
are leaving me.
The lovely freezing passions,
tickle lonely nights,
Lost nights, empty nights.

I am coming into the world.
I am approaching with a smile.

THE EARLY SPRING

The world has come alive with beauty.
Listen very carefully,
You can hear the beautiful silence of an
    early spring.
The sun shines brightly down on god's
    lands
Making all things new again.

The birds sing softly to themselves,
But loud enough so others can hear.
The winds blow gently,
Lightly skimming the trees,
But making a quiet gently breeze.

The ocean wails in the distance with
It's rolling waves and lonely beach.
You can hear it if you listen very closely.

Can you feel the warmth?
Can you hear the spring?
Can you see the beauty?

It's all there waiting for me and you.

SEARCHING

What have we searched for?
And what have we found?

We searched for happiness,
Love, security, belonging
And an answer to our loneliness.

We found our happiness
within each other.
We found our love, a special kind of
 love
We found security
I found a sense of belonging
A kind I never had.

Did we find any answers?
I found more questions.
There will never be an answer
To my loneliness.
I've searched long and hard
Down rocky roads

Why stop now?
There's more out in the world
Than meets the eye.
I will find it all
Without your help
without your guidance.

I can always make it alone

But I don't always want to.

THE TRAVELLER

I have travelled to many places,
met many people of all kinds
and experienced a lot in life
loving and growing
with each experience.

Seeing the beauty of
The countryside,
Discovering something new each day.
Being so much into my mind
And so much aware of inside meaning.

I met a philosopher once,
While in my travels.
He was wise and kind.
The knowledge he gave me
Has always been with me
And is helping me through each step I
      take
In life, love and reality.

I often take a wrong turn
And find myself entangled in fears
Searching for a new road
To let me experience, grow and learn.

ROSE COLORED GLASSES

I see through the rose colored glasses
At one who has never seen me.

The world perceived through
Rose colored glasses
Is one of great beauty
Immensity beyond all imagination.

A place you will never be again
A place that would never allow you in.

The colors and laughter
The joy in the air
All can be seen through
Rose colored glasses.

I saw a light dim through
The broken dreams
And I felt a new and meaningful
Friendship breaks through.

I perceived you as one original
I never thought one human being
Could care so much.

You see me as myself
You understand my depth and purpose
I understand your meaning.

TAKE ME AWAY

Take me far away on a magical trip
Everywhere from sun to sea
Take me to those places
I cannot foresee.
Take me where I want to be

Living, loving and laughing
Can keep you going strong
If you live to the fullest
Love will make you stronger.

You have the basic recipe
For happiness, fulfillment and joy
So let's stay on this course
A little longer.

Go a little further in life
Keep our values and stand our ground.

JUNGLE OF HOPE

Slipping through the jungles of hope
I find myself entangled in a web
Of utter isolation and fear
The things I long for
I cannot reach
The love I hope for
I cannot see.

The happiness I search for
I hope I'll find.
Peace of mind is a goal
While running through the maze of life.

Taking each twist and corner with care
Finding discouragement in dead ends
And hope in a beam of light
Shining from the distance.

Stumbling through the darkness
I found myself.

MY CHILD

I feel a slight uneasiness inside me
As the thoughts flow through my brain.
I feel pain and guilt; fear and shame.

I believe there is a growing miracle
        inside me
That takes each breath from mine.
One who could bring me
Great joy and love.

I think about the dreams for my child
Love & Understanding
Support and encouragement.

I want to watch my child grow
And learn experience and discover.
I want to be by his side
In times of frustration and confusion.

There is so much I want for my child
That I just can't possibly give
Yet I'll be there every step of the way
With all the love I have.

ALONE

It seems we are born into this world
      ALONE
with only the love and support of our
      parents.
As we grow, friends become more
      important
Dependency on others grows...as we
      grow.

Life has many twists and turns
Road which are difficult to decide
Decisions which reap full consequences
We may believe that marriage and
      children
Will take the loneliness away
But life is here to stay

We are all alone in this world
No one experiences, feels or thinks
Like we do.
No one can truly understand the life
      you lead
No one can walk in your shoes.

After all we are individuals and
Many go through life alone
We are born into this world alone
And we leave this world alone.

If you have a loved one to walk this life with
Remember to be grateful for that.

THE MOUNTAINTOP

Sitting here upon my rock
Listening to the sound of nothingness.
The sun slowly sinks behind the clouds
Misty orange, pink and grey.

Crickets hum to the tune of the sun
As ducks make their way across the
    pond
Cows slowly trod to the haven of their
    barn
As spiders busily weave their webs for
    the night.

What a peaceful place, this mountain
of ours
Fields and trees forever, waterfalls and
streams
Still lives in this place.

Mountains still nurture the land
The land still nurtures the people.
And all of nature and man
Live is a peaceful harmony here.

The clouds are sinking faster now
Soon – the night will fall
The starts will shine so brightly
In this clear mountain sky.

This place holds a familiar sense of calm

And seems to have taken hold of my
        soul.
It inspires my mind to the fullest
And has captured my heart.

I feel it should slowly bring out the
Best of my mind, body and soul.
As all the creatures, big and small
Nestle down for the night.

So shall I, in my new mountain nest.

THE DISTANCE

In the dusk of the evening,
As the sun melts behind the clouds in
    the sky,
The thoughts in my mind drift tenderly
    to you.

I can see your face in my mind
I can see your eyes, which shine the light
    of love.
I can see your tears, which remind me
    of your sorrow.
I can see your smile, which fills my life
    with hope.

No matter how far the distance is
    between us,
No matter how many miles away you
    are from me,
I can feel your presence here – strong
    and reassuring
I can feel your love here – powerful
    and overwhelming.

As the darkness of the evening creeps
    on,
The emptiness and quiet surrounds me.
As I stumble on to sleep
In my dreams I'll be thinking of you.

Printed in Great Britain
by Amazon